CORNING®

FRESH FLAVOURS OF SPRING

CONTENTS

STARTERS

Portobello Mushroom, Prosciutto and Parmesan Crostini 3
Antipasto Salad 4
Black Bean Salad with Seafood 7
Pizza Bagel Melt 8
Roasted Veggie Wrap 11

MAINS

Chicken with Marsala 12
Richly Flavoured Quiche 15
Vegetable Pasta Gratin 16
Fish and Crab Cakes with Tartar Sauce 19
Artichoke, Mushroom and Cheese Frittata 20
Stuffed Chicken Breasts 23
Quick Brunch Wrap 24
Pasta with Spring Flavours 27
Spaghettini with White Clam Sauce 28
Sliced Cold Beef Tenderloin with Horseradish Sauce 31
Pasta with a Passion 32
Baked Penne in Spicy Cream Sauce 32
Butterflied Leg of Lamb 35
Shrimp with Tomato and Feta 36
Cornish Hens with Lime Herb Rub 39
Ham and Cheese Breakfast Strata 40

SIDES

Oven-baked Risotto with Mushrooms and Asparagus 43
Beets with Mustard and Tarragon 44
Make-ahead Mashed Potatoes with a Hint of Garlic 47
Tropical Salad with Poppy Seed Dressing 48
Fragrant Basmati Rice Pilaf 51
Caesar Salad 52

DESSERTS

Rhubarb Custard Pie in Phyllo 55
White Chocolate Tart with Fruit 56
Lemon Poppy Seed Cake 59
Blueberry Cobbler 60
Tart Lemon Triangles 63

Portobello Mushroom, Prosciutto and Parmesan Crostini

Crostini make really satisfying before-dinner starters. This delectable combination could easily make a meal for two.

Makes 6 servings.

4	*large portobello mushrooms*	4
¼ cup	*olive oil*	50 mL
3 tbsp	*balsamic vinegar*	45 mL
2	*garlic cloves, minced*	2
	salt and pepper, to taste	
¼ lb	*prosciutto*	125 g
1	*baguette, sliced and toasted*	1
	Parmesan cheese, shaved	
	fresh basil leaves, finely sliced, for garnish	

1. Remove stems from mushrooms and put mushroom caps in a glass baking dish, smooth side down. Mix together oil, vinegar, garlic and salt and pepper and pour over the mushrooms. Marinate for 1 hour.
2. Preheat oven to 400°F (200°C). Roast mushrooms in marinade until tender, about 10 minutes. Remove from oven and chop mushrooms into small pieces.
3. Place thin slice of prosciutto on top of each piece of toasted bread then spoon mushroom mixture on top. Sprinkle with Parmesan cheese and broil until cheese melts. Garnish with basil leaves.

CORNING RECOMMENDS

PYREX® ORIGINALS™ OVENWARE 2-qt Oblong Baking Dish and CORNINGWARE® Casual Elegance White Flora™ Oval Platter

Antipasto Salad

Serve with grilled meats as part of an appetizer tray. Garnish the platter with lettuce leaves, dill sprigs and red pepper strips.

Makes 6–8 servings.

1	*can (19 oz/540 mL) chick peas, drained and rinsed*	1
1	*small jar marinated artichoke hearts (not drained), diced*	1
½ lb	*feta cheese, diced*	500 g
1	*roasted red pepper, peeled and diced*	1
½ cup	*black olives*	125 mL
1	*garlic clove, minced*	1
¼ cup	*lemon juice*	50 mL
1 tsp	*Dijon mustard*	5 mL
¼ tsp	*oregano*	1 mL
¾ cup	*vegetable oil or olive oil*	175 mL
½ cup	*chopped fresh dill or basil leaves*	125 mL
	salt and pepper, to taste	

1. Combine chick peas, artichoke hearts, cheese, pepper and olives in a large bowl.
2. In a small mixing bowl, stir together garlic, lemon juice, mustard and oregano. Whisk in oil. Add dill or basil.
3. Pour dressing over cheese and vegetable mixture. Toss well. Let stand at least 30 minutes before serving. Antipasto can be made several hours or up to 2 days ahead. Toss well before serving. Adjust seasoning with salt and pepper.

CORNING RECOMMENDS

Blush Blue SCULPTURED™ PYREX® Serving Bowl and CORELLE® IMPRESSIONS® Enhancements Serving Platter

Black Bean Salad with Seafood

This salad has Mexican-style flavours and makes a great beginning to a meal on a hot summer's night with friends on the patio!
Makes 6–8 servings.

1	*can (19 oz/540 mL) black beans, drained and rinsed*	1
½ cup	*finely diced red onion*	125 mL
2	*green onions, chopped*	2
1	*yellow pepper, diced*	1
2	*corn cobs, niblets removed or 1 cup (250 mL) frozen corn niblets*	2
2	*avocados, diced*	2
8 oz	*seafood of choice: flaked crab meat, lobster, smoked salmon or shrimp*	250 g
¼ cup	*fresh cilantro or parsley, chopped*	50 mL
¼ cup	*lime juice*	50 mL
2 tbsp	*olive oil*	30 mL
	salt and pepper, to taste	
6–8	*small tomatoes, cut in sixths or hollowed out*	6–8
	fresh cilantro or parsley, for garnish	

1. In a large mixing bowl, combine all ingredients, except tomatoes and garnish. Toss well and refrigerate for 1 hour.
2. To serve, spoon salad around or into tomatoes. Garnish with fresh cilantro or parsley.

Pizza Bagel Melt

Everybody loves pizza and bagels, so why not eat them together?

Makes 4 servings.

¼ cup	*sun-dried tomatoes*	50 mL
4	*marinated artichoke hearts, bottled*	4
4	*bagels, sliced in half*	4
1 cup	*pasta sauce, homemade or store bought*	250 mL
2 cups	*grated mozzarella cheese*	500 mL
¼ cup	*shredded fresh basil leaves*	50 mL
½ cup	*sliced mushrooms*	125 mL

1. Preheat oven to 350°F (180°C).
2. Soak sun-dried tomatoes in hot water for 20 minutes. Drain and thinly slice. Chop artichoke hearts.
3. Put bagels, cut side up, in a single layer in a 9 × 13-inch (3.5-L) baking dish. Spread sauce on each bagel. Sprinkle on mozzarella, dividing the cheese evenly among the bagels. Add the basil, mushrooms, tomatoes and artichoke hearts.
4. Bake for 10 to 15 minutes until cheese is bubbly. Cut each bagel half into quarters to serve.

CORNING RECOMMENDS

PYREX® Originals 3-qt Oblong Baking Dish, CORELLE® IMPRESSIONS® Sand Art 12 ¼" Serving Platter and Salad/Dessert Plate

Roasted Veggie Wrap

This can be an appetizer or a great casual dinner dish for the vegetarians in the crowd! **Makes 4 servings.**

3 tbsp	*olive oil*	45 mL
2 tbsp	*balsamic vinegar*	30 mL
1	*garlic clove, minced*	1
1 tsp	*oregano*	5 mL
2	*small zucchini, sliced*	2
1	*yellow pepper, sliced*	1
2	*Portobello mushrooms, sliced*	2
2	*tomatoes, cut into wedges*	2
4	*large flour tortillas*	4
1 cup	*feta cheese, crumbled*	250 mL
1	*large red onion, thinly sliced*	1

1. Preheat oven to 350°F (180°C).
2. Mix oil, vinegar, garlic and oregano together and toss with the sliced zucchini, pepper, mushrooms and tomatoes. Place mixture in a baking dish and roast for 25 minutes, stirring occasionally.
3. Wrap tortillas in foil and put them in the oven to warm for the last 15 minutes that the vegetables are cooking.
4. To serve, divide the vegetables evenly among the four tortillas, sprinkle the feta and red onion evenly on top of the vegetables. For each tortilla, fold one end over the vegetables, then fold the sides over the vegetables. Place seam side down on a plate.

CORNING RECOMMENDS

PYREX® Originals™ 3-qt Oblong Baking Dish and CORELLE® IMPRESSIONS® Callaway Dinner Plate

Chicken with Marsala

This dish is an elegant entrée, sure to be appreciated by dinner guests.
Makes 6 servings.

¼ cup	*unsalted butter*	50 mL
6	*single, boneless, skinless chicken breasts*	6
½ lb	*mushrooms, sliced*	250 g
3	*medium red onions, thinly sliced*	3
2	*garlic cloves, chopped*	2
1 cup	*chicken stock, homemade or canned*	250 mL
½ tsp	*dried rosemary*	2 mL
½ tsp	*dried thyme*	2 mL
⅓ cup	*Marsala wine*	75 mL
1 cup	*heavy cream*	250 mL
	salt and pepper, to taste	
¼ cup	*chopped parsley*	50 mL

1. Heat 2 tbsp (30 mL) butter in a large skillet. Pat chicken breasts dry and put in skillet. Brown on each side. Arrange in a single layer in a shallow casserole. Add mushrooms to pan and cook over medium-high heat until just cooked. Spoon over chicken breasts.
2. Add remaining butter to pan. Cook onions, garlic, and ½ cup (125 mL) stock until onions are very soft, about 15 minutes. Stir in rosemary and thyme. Purée onion mixture and reserve.
3. Turn heat to high. Add remaining stock and Marsala to pan. Add cream. Reduce over high heat 5 minutes.
4. Stir onion purée into sauce. Season with salt and pepper. Pour sauce over chicken. Sprinkle with parsley.
5. Cover and bake in a preheated 350°F (180°C) oven for 35 minutes or until mixture is bubbling. Remove cover during last 10 minutes.

Richly Flavoured Quiche

Quiche is a lovely choice for a spring lunch or brunch and this one can be easily made. **Makes 6–8 servings.**

1	*10-inch (25-cm) pastry shell*	1
2 tbsp	*unsalted butter*	30 mL
2	*red peppers, diced*	2
2	*garlic cloves, finely chopped*	2
10	*green onions, cut in ½-inch (1-cm) pieces*	10
½ lb	*chèvre, crumbled*	250 g
3	*eggs*	3
1 ¼ cups	*sour cream*	300 mL
½ tsp	*salt*	2 mL
¼ tsp	*pepper*	1 mL
2 tbsp	*shredded fresh basil*	30 mL

1. Preheat oven to 425°F (225°C). Line shell with parchment or foil. Fill with dried beans or pie weight. Bake at 425°F (225°C) for 15 to 20 minutes until golden and almost cooked. If pastry still seems raw at base, return to oven for 3 to 4 minutes. Reduce heat to 350°F (180°C).
2. Heat butter over medium heat in large skillet. Add peppers and garlic and cook until very soft but not brown, about 8 minutes. Add onions and cook another 4 minutes. Cool mixture slightly then spread over pastry. Sprinkle chèvre over top.
3. Lightly beat eggs. Stir in sour cream, salt, pepper and basil. Pour over filling and gently mix in with fork.
4. Bake at 350°F (180°C) for 35 to 40 minutes until golden and centre is firm. Let stand 10 minutes before serving.

CORNING RECOMMENDS

PYREX® Originals™ 1-pt Measuring Cup and CORNINGWARE® FRENCH WHITE® 10" Pie Plate

Vegetable Pasta Gratin

This is a good choice for a vegetarian menu.
Makes 4 servings.

5 tbsp	*olive oil*	75 mL
2	*garlic cloves, minced*	2
1/4 tsp	*dried pepper flakes*	1 mL
1	*can (28 oz/796 mL) plum tomatoes, puréed*	1
	salt and pepper, to taste	
1/4 cup	*chopped fresh basil*	50 mL
2	*medium red onions, coarsely chopped*	2
3	*medium zucchini, sliced*	3
1	*bulb fennel, coarsely chopped*	1
	salt and pepper, to taste	
1 lb	*dried pasta (such as penne or orecchiette)*	500 g
1/3 cup	*chopped parsley*	75 mL
1 cup	*grated mozzarella or fontina cheese*	250 mL
1/2 cup	*grated Parmesan Reggiano cheese*	125 mL

1. To prepare tomato sauce, heat 2 tbsp (30 mL) oil in saucepan and cook garlic until softened. Add pepper flakes and tomatoes. Cook, uncovered, for 30 minutes until thickened. Remove from heat. Season with salt and pepper. Stir in basil. Set aside.
2. In a large bowl, toss onions, zucchini and fennel with 3 tbsp (45 mL) oil. Spread mixture in one layer in a large oiled baking dish. Roast at 400°F (200°C) until golden, about 30 minutes. Stir occasionally. Season with salt and pepper.
3. Cook pasta until just tender. Drain well. Lightly oil a shallow ovenproof dish. Assemble gratin by layering tomato sauce, pasta, vegetables and parsley. Top with mozzarella and Parmesan.
4. Bake at 350°F (180°C) for 35 to 40 minutes, or until bubbly around the edges. Let stand 5 minutes before serving.

Put One Away

Double the recipe and assemble one dish of the gratin in a freezer-proof casserole dish. Freeze. Thaw overnight in refrigerator and bake as instructed.

Fish and Crab Cakes with Tartar Sauce

These make a tasty meal with some crunchy potatoes and a fresh green salad.
Makes 4 servings.

Tartar Sauce

1 cup	*mayonnaise*	250 mL
2	*gherkin pickles, finely chopped*	2
2 tbsp	*capers, drained*	30 mL
1	*green onion, finely chopped*	1
2 tbsp	*chopped parsley*	30 mL
2 tbsp	*lemon juice*	30 mL
½ tsp	*tarragon*	2 mL
	salt and pepper, to taste	

1 lb	*cooked fish (such as halibut, snapper, cod or salmon)*	500 g
4 oz	*crab meat, defrosted and flaked*	115 g
1 cup	*cooked mashed potatoes*	250 mL
½ cup	*bread crumbs*	125 mL
1	*egg, beaten*	1
¼ cup	*chopped green onions*	50 mL
¼ cup	*chopped fresh parsley*	50 mL
2 tbsp	*mayonnaise*	30 mL
1 tbsp	*Dijon mustard*	15 mL
1 tbsp	*capers, drained and chopped*	15 mL
1 tsp	*Worcestershire sauce*	5 mL
1 tsp	*salt*	5 mL
⅛ tsp	*freshly ground black pepper, or to taste*	0.5 mL
¼ tsp	*Tabasco*	1 mL
	butter or oil for cooking	

1. To prepare tartar sauce, combine all ingredients and mix well. Adjust seasonings if necessary. Sauce is best prepared several hours ahead of time to let flavours blend. Keep sauce refrigerated.
2. To prepare fish cakes, flake cooked fish and add the remaining fish cake ingredients except butter. Mix well to combine ingredients thoroughly.
3. Shape into large or small patties. Heat butter or oil in a large skillet and cook 3 to 5 minutes per side until nicely browned and heated thoroughly. Drain on paper towels if necessary. Serve hot or cold with tartar sauce.

Artichoke, Mushroom and Cheese Frittata

This really is a quiche without the crust and it's a tasty dish for a special lunch or brunch.

Makes 4–6 servings.

2 tbsp	*butter*	30 mL
1	*medium onion, chopped*	1
½ lb	*mushrooms, thinly sliced*	250 g
5	*whole eggs*	5
3 tbsp	*water*	45 mL
	salt and pepper, to taste	
2 tbsp	*chopped parsley*	30 mL
1	*jar (6 oz/175 g) marinated artichoke hearts, chopped*	1
4 oz	*grated old cheddar cheese*	115 g
3 oz	*chèvre, crumbled*	85 g
½ cup	*fresh bread crumbs*	125 mL

1. Melt butter in a large skillet. Cook onion and mushrooms until soft and all liquid has evaporated. Cool slightly.
2. In a large bowl, stir eggs until yolks and whites are blended. Add water, seasonings and parsley. Stir in artichokes, cheeses and bread crumbs.
3. Pour into a buttered 9-inch (23-cm) square baking dish. Bake at 375°F (190°C) for 30 to 35 minutes or until eggs are set. Let stand at least 10 minutes before serving.

CORNING RECOMMENDS

PYREX® Originals™ 8-inch Square Cake Dish and CORELLE® IMPRESSIONS® Sand Art Dinner Plate

Stuffed Chicken Breasts

This is so easy but it always looks beautiful and tastes wonderful!
Makes 8 servings.

1 tbsp	*butter*	15 mL
1	*small onion, finely chopped*	1
1 pkg	*fresh spinach, chopped*	1 pkg
2 cups	*ricotta cheese*	500 mL
¼ tsp	*salt*	1 mL
	pinch of pepper	
½ tsp	*dried basil*	2 mL
8	*single, boneless chicken breasts, skin on*	8

1. Preheat oven to 350°F (180°C).
2. Heat butter over medium heat in a large skillet. Add onion and cook until soft, about 4 minutes. Add spinach and cook for about 2 minutes, until spinach has wilted and the moisture evaporates. Combine mixture with the ricotta cheese, salt, pepper and basil in a food processor and pulse four or five times to blend.
3. Trim excess fat from chicken breast. Loosen the skin from one side of the breast and stuff ¼ cup (50 mL) of the ricotta mixture under the skin. Tuck the loose skin under the breast, forming a round dome shape. Repeat with remaining breasts. Put the stuffed breasts close together in a buttered baking dish. Brush with melted butter.
4. Bake breasts until golden brown, about 35 minutes.
5. Chicken breasts can be served whole or cooled to room temperature and sliced into four pieces each for a pretty presentation.

CORNING RECOMMENDS

PYREX® Originals™
3-qt Oblong Baking Dish

Quick Brunch Wrap

This could be called bacon-and-eggs-to-go!
Makes 4 servings.

16	*slices of bacon, cut into small pieces*	16
1	*small onion, finely chopped*	1
8	*eggs*	8
8 tbsp	*water*	120 mL
	generous grinding of black pepper	
	Tabasco sauce, to taste	
4	*large flour tortillas*	4

1. Sauté bacon pieces in a nonstick frying pan until crispy. Remove from pan and pour off all but 1 tsp (5 mL) of the drippings. Add onion and sauté for 5 minutes.
2. Put eggs into a bowl and lightly whisk with the water and pepper. Pour eggs into the pan with the onion and cook over medium heat, stirring frequently. Just before eggs are done, stir in the cooked bacon and sprinkle on Tabasco, to taste.
3. Warm the tortillas on a plate in the microwave for 20 seconds or wrapped in foil in a 350°F (180°C) oven for 15 minutes.
4. To serve, divide the egg mixture evenly among the 4 tortillas. Fold one end of each tortilla over the eggs, then fold the sides over the eggs. Place seam side down on a plate to serve.

Pasta with Spring Flavours

Pasta can — and should — be enjoyed every season. This version, with asparagus and peas, is a light and tasty addition to a spring menu.

Makes 4 servings.

2 tbsp	*olive oil*	30 mL
½ lb	*mushrooms, thinly sliced*	250 g
2	*garlic cloves, minced*	2
½ lb	*asparagus, cut in 1-inch (2.5-cm) lengths*	250 g
½ lb	*sugar snap peas*	250 g
½ cup	*dry white wine*	125 mL
1 cup	*chicken stock*	250 mL
2 tbsp	*diced sun-dried tomatoes*	30 mL
1 lb	*pasta bows, fusilli or penne*	500 g
¼ cup	*chopped fresh dill*	175 mL
¼ cup	*pine nuts, toasted**	175 mL
	salt and pepper to taste	

* Toast pine nuts in 350° F (180°C) oven for 6 minutes, or just starting to colour.

1. Heat oil in a large skillet. Add mushrooms, garlic and asparagus. Sauté over high heat for 3 minutes. Add peas, wine, stock and tomatoes. Reduce heat to medium and cook 5 to 7 minutes, or until vegetables are tender crisp.
2. While vegetables are cooking, cook pasta in a large amount of boiling water until al dente. Drain pasta and place in a large serving bowl.
3. Add vegetables, dill and pine nuts to pasta. Season with salt and pepper. Toss well. Serve.

Spaghettini with White Clam Sauce

This is a favourite restaurant dish that you can easily make at home!
Makes 4 servings.

¼ cup	*extra virgin olive oil*	50 mL
2	*garlic cloves, finely chopped*	2
3	*green onions, finely chopped*	3
¼ tsp	*hot red chili flakes*	1 mL
2 tbsp	*chopped fresh parsley*	30 mL
¼ tsp	*dried oregano*	1 mL
2	*cans (5 oz/142 g each) baby clams (well drained, liquid reserved)*	2
⅓ cup	*dry white wine*	75 mL
	freshly ground black pepper, to taste	
1 lb	*spaghettini*	500 g
1 tsp	*cornstarch*	5 mL
2 tbsp	*cold water*	30 mL
2 tbsp	*unsalted butter*	30 mL
2 tbsp	*chopped fresh parsley*	30 mL
¼ cup	*chopped fresh basil*	50 mL
	salt, to taste	

1. Heat oil in a large skillet and cook garlic, onions and chili flakes until tender and fragrant but do not brown.
2. Add parsley, oregano and clams and cook 2 minutes longer.
3. Add clam juice, white wine and pepper. Reduce slightly to concentrate flavours. Remove from heat until spaghettini is ready.
4. Cook spaghettini in a large pot of boiling salted water. Reheat sauce just before pasta is cooked. Combine cornstarch with water and stir into sauce. Cook only until slightly thickened.
5. Drain pasta well. Do not rinse. Toss with butter and sauce. Sprinkle with parsley and basil. Add salt only if necessary. Serve immediately.

CORNING RECOMMENDS

REVERE® 10-inch Skillet and CORELLE® IMPRESSIONS® Enhancements 20oz Salad/Pasta Bowl

Sliced Cold Beef Tenderloin with Horseradish Sauce

Beef tenderloin is a special treat for family or friends, and when you taste this, you'll agree it's worth it!
Makes 6 servings.

¼ cup	*Dijon mustard*	50 mL
2 tbsp	*soya sauce*	30 mL
2 tbsp	*crushed green peppercorns*	30 mL
2 tbsp	*olive oil*	30 mL
2 lb	*beef tenderloin, trimmed and tied if necessary*	1 kg
4 cups	*Boston lettuce leaves*	1 L
½ cup	*mayonnaise*	125 mL
¼ cup	*sour cream or yogurt*	50 mL
1 tbsp	*Dijon mustard*	15 mL
2 tsp	*horseradish, or more to taste*	10 mL
	salt and pepper	

1. Combine mustard, soya sauce, peppercorns and olive oil and rub into meat. Let stand 30 minutes.
2. Place beef on a roasting rack. Roast for 20 minutes at 425°F (225°C). Reduce heat to 350°F (180°C) and continue roasting for 20 to 25 minutes or until meat thermometer registers 140°F (60°C) for medium rare.
3. Let meat cool to room temperature. Refrigerate for several hours, or overnight.
4. Slice meat thinly and arrange on lettuce-lined serving platter.
5. Combine mayonnaise, sour cream, mustard, horseradish and salt and pepper, and drizzle over meat.

CORNING RECOMMENDS

PYREX® ORIGINALS™ 3-qt Oblong Baking Dish and CORELLE® IMPRESSIONS® Fresh Cut 12 ¼" Serving Platter and Salad/Dessert Plate

Pasta with a Passion

If you can take the heat, increase the amount of red pepper flakes!
Makes 4 servings.

¼ cup	*olive oil*	50 mL
1	*large onion, sliced*	1
4	*garlic cloves, minced*	4
½ tsp	*crushed red pepper flakes*	2 mL
1	*can (28 oz/796 mL) plum tomatoes with juices*	1
	salt, to taste	
1 lb	*orecchiette or penne*	500 g
2 tbsp	*chopped basil*	30 mL

1. Heat oil in a saucepan over low heat. Cook onion, garlic and pepper flakes about 5 minutes. Add tomatoes, cover and simmer for 20 minutes. Put sauce in a food processor and purée. Stir in salt.
2. Cook penne in boiling salted water until al dente, about 10 minutes. Drain, toss with sauce and sprinkle with basil.

Put One Away

Double the recipe and assemble one dish of the pasta in a freezer-proof casserole dish. Freeze. Thaw overnight in refrigerator and bake as instructed.

Baked Penne in Spicy Cream Sauce

1 lb	*penne*	500 g
2 cups	*Pasta with a Passion sauce (above)*	500 mL
½ cup	*whipping cream*	125 mL
1 ½ cups	*grated Parmesan cheese*	375 mL

1. Cook penne in boiling salted water for half the usual time.
2. Stir cream into sauce and add 1 cup (250 mL) Parmesan cheese and the penne. Put mixture into a buttered casserole dish. Sprinkle with remaining cheese and bake at 425°F (225°C) for 10 minutes.

CORNING RECOMMENDS

PYREX® Originals™ 1-pt Measuring Cup and CORELLE® IMPRESSIONS® Summer Blush Soup Bowls and Dinner Plate

Butterflied Leg of Lamb

A nice long marinating time will produce lamb gently flavoured with garlic and rosemary. Serve a Greek salad on the side with roasted potatoes for a Mediterranean-style feast.

Makes 6 servings.

4 lb	*leg of lamb, butterflied*	2 kg
2 tbsp	*Dijon mustard*	30 mL
2 tbsp	*honey*	30 mL
4	*garlic cloves, minced*	4
2 tbsp	*balsamic vinegar*	30 mL
½ cup	*olive oil*	175 mL
1 tsp	*rosemary*	5 mL
½ tsp	*salt*	2 mL
¼ tsp	*freshly ground pepper*	1 mL

1. Trim excess fat from lamb. Combine remaining ingredients. Rub into lamb. Marinate lamb several hours (or overnight) in refrigerator.
2. To cook lamb, roast uncovered, fat side up in preheated 375°F (190°C) oven for 30 minutes for medium, or longer if you prefer well done. Baste several times during cooking. Let lamb stand in warm place for 10 minutes before carving.

CORNING RECOMMENDS

Clear Sculptured PYREX® Ovenware
4 ½-qt Salad Bowl with Storage Cover

Shrimp with Tomato and Feta

This dish has Greek overtones, with its olive oil, garlic, oregano and feta. It's tasty, quick and easy to make!

Makes 4–6 servings.

3 tbsp	*olive oil*	45 mL
1	*onion, chopped*	1
2	*garlic cloves, minced*	2
1	*can (28 oz/796 mL) plum tomatoes, drained and chopped, juices reserved*	1
¼ cup	*chopped parsley*	50 mL
½ tsp	*oregano*	2 mL
	freshly ground pepper, to taste	
1 ½ lb	*shrimp, peeled and deveined*	750 g
½ lb	*feta cheese, crumbled*	250 g

1. Heat oil in a large skillet. Add onion and garlic and cook until soft but not browned. Add tomatoes, parsley, oregano and pepper. Cook until thickened, about 8 minutes. If mixture seems too thick, add some of the reserved juices.
2. Add shrimp to sauce and cook 2 minutes.
3. Pour mixture into a shallow casserole. Sprinkle with feta. Bake in a preheated 425°F (225°C) oven for 15 minutes, or until cheese melts. Serve hot with crusty bread, pasta or rice.

CORNING RECOMMENDS

CORNINGWARE® FRENCH WHITE® 2 ½-qt Oval Casserole and CORELLE® IMPRESSIONS® Callaway 20oz Salad/Pasta Bowl and Dinner Plate

Cornish Hens with Lime Herb Rub

Rubs are popular ways to marinate poultry, pork or red meat. By "rubbing" the mixture of herbs and spices into the meat, the flavours become more intense than the usual marinating. This piquant combination of herbs and lime has a lovely fresh flavour. **Makes 6 servings.**

1 cup	*parsley leaves*	250 mL
1 cup	*cilantro leaves*	250 mL
3	*garlic cloves*	3
1 tsp	*dried oregano or 1 tbsp (15 mL) fresh*	5 mL
2 tbsp	*sesame seeds*	30 mL
	grated zest from 2 limes	
⅓ cup	*lime juice*	75 mL
½ tsp	*hot chili paste or pinch of cayenne*	2 mL
⅓ cup	*honey*	75 mL
⅓ cup	*olive oil*	75 mL
½ tsp	*salt*	2 mL
¼ tsp	*pepper*	1 mL
3	*Cornish hens, split in half with backbone removed*	3

1. To prepare the rub, finely chop parsley, cilantro and garlic in food processor. Add oregano, sesame seeds, lime zest and juice, chili paste, honey, olive oil, salt and pepper and blend together.
2. Spread one-half of the mixture over the hens and rub it in. Marinate in the refrigerator for at least 2 hours, up to 12 hours.
3. Place hens, skin side up, in a roasting pan. Roast in a preheated 375°F (190°C) oven for 35 minutes, or until juices run clear when tested at thigh. Baste chicken a few times during cooking. Serve with remaining rub in a side dish.

Ham and Cheese Breakfast Strata

This is a perfect brunch dish. You can make the egg mixture ahead of time and refrigerate it until you want to combine it with the bread cubes. Memorable! **Makes 6 servings.**

6	*slices multigrain or seed bread*	6
2 tbsp	*soft butter*	30 mL
6 oz	*Black Forest ham, cut in small cubes*	175 g
1 ½ cups	*grated Gruyère cheese*	375 mL
1 cup	*grated old cheddar cheese*	250 mL
2 tbsp	*chopped sun-dried tomatoes*	30 mL
2 tbsp	*chopped parsley*	30 mL
2	*green onions, chopped*	2
4	*eggs*	4
2 ¼ cups	*milk*	550 mL
½ tsp	*dry mustard*	2 mL
½ tsp	*Worcestershire sauce*	2 mL
½ tsp	*salt*	2 mL
	pepper, to taste	

1. Spread bread with butter. Cut into 1-inch (2.5-cm) cubes. Put in a bowl and combine with ham, both cheeses, tomatoes, parsley and onions.
2. In a mixing bowl, whisk eggs until blended. Add milk, mustard, Worcestershire sauce, salt and pepper.
3. Pour milk mixture over bread. Stir to combine. Pour into a buttered 11 × 7-inch (2-L) baking dish.
4. Place dish on foil-lined baking sheet. Bake in a preheated 350°F (180°C) oven for 50 to 60 minutes until golden and puffed. Let stand 10 minutes before serving.

CORNING RECOMMENDS

PYREX® Originals™ 1-pt Measuring Cup and PYREX® Originals™ 2-qt Oblong Baking Dish with CORELLE® IMPRESSIONS® Oceanview Salad/Dessert Plates

Oven-baked Risotto with Mushrooms and Asparagus

Many risotto recipes call for careful stovetop cooking but this one is easily done in the oven. Serve with Stuffed Chicken Breasts, page 23, for a special occasion. **Makes 4 servings.**

2 tbsp	*butter*	30 mL
1	*large onion, thinly sliced*	1
1 tbsp	*olive oil*	15 mL
½ lb	*fresh mushrooms, sliced*	250 g
2	*garlic cloves, finely minced*	2
1 cup	*rice (not instant)*	250 mL
2 ¼ cups	*chicken broth*	550 mL
¼ cup	*dry white wine*	50 mL
1 tsp	*salt*	2 mL
¼ tsp	*white pepper*	1 mL
½ lb	*asparagus, tips only*	250 g
¼ cup	*grated Parmesan cheese*	50 mL
	chopped parsley, for garnish	

1. Preheat oven to 325°F (160°C), with empty casserole in oven to warm.
2. In a skillet, heat butter and sauté onion until tender. Remove onion from pan and set aside. Heat oil and sauté mushrooms and garlic until tender. Return onion to pan.
3. Add rice and stir well to coat with butter. Add broth, wine, salt and pepper. Transfer to warmed casserole and cover.
4. Bake for 15 minutes. Add asparagus and stir. Cover and return to oven. Cook for 10 to 15 minutes, or until rice is cooked. Remove from oven. Stir in Parmesan and sprinkle with parsley.

Beets with Mustard and Tarragon

Beets add such beautiful colour to a meal and their taste is so wholesome!
Makes 4–6 servings.

1 ½ lb	*beets*	750 g
1 tbsp	*coarse-grain mustard*	15 mL
2 tbsp	*balsamic vinegar*	30 mL
2 tbsp	*olive oil*	30 mL
1 tbsp	*chopped fresh tarragon or 1 tsp/5 mL dried*	15 mL
	salt and pepper, to taste	

1. Trim beet greens. Wash beets well. Place in 2 ½-qt (2.5-L) saucepan. Cover with water. Bring to boil, reduce heat and cook 25 to 40 minutes (depending on size) until tender. Drain and let cool until you can handle them. Peel beets and cut into slices or wedges.
2. Stir together mustard, vinegar, oil and tarragon. Pour over beets. Season with salt and pepper. Toss and serve hot or at room temperature.

CORNING RECOMMENDS
PYREX® STORAGE PLUS®
7-cup Round Bowls

Make-ahead Mashed Potatoes with a Hint of Garlic

Everybody loves mashed potatoes but they're inconvenient for the cook who has other things to do before dinner besides mashing potatoes. This fits the bill both ways — so delicious tasting and it can be prepared ahead of time.

Makes 6–8 servings.

8–10	*potatoes, peeled and cut into chunks*	8–10
8 oz	*garlic-and-herb-flavoured cream cheese*	250 g
1 cup	*sour cream*	250 mL
1 cup	*milk or light cream*	250 mL
¼ cup	*finely chopped green onions*	50 mL
1 tsp	*salt*	5 mL
	white pepper, to taste (optional)	
	paprika, for garnish	

1. Boil potatoes until soft but not mushy. Drain well.
2. Mash potatoes in the pot they're cooked in. Once they are smooth, incorporate cream cheese, sour cream and milk, beating well after each addition. Stir in onions, salt and white pepper (if using).
3. Spoon mixture into a well-greased 2-qt (2-L) casserole dish and sprinkle with paprika. Casserole can be refrigerated or baked immediately at 350°F (180°C) for 30 minutes.

CORNING RECOMMENDS

PYREX® Cranberry 2-qt Knob Covered Casserole

Tropical Salad with Poppy Seed Dressing

Light and refreshing and a nice change from the usual tossed greens.
Makes 8 servings.

¾ cup	*olive oil*	175 mL
¼ cup	*red wine vinegar*	50 mL
2 tbsp	*lemon juice*	30 mL
2 tbsp	*honey*	30 mL
1 tbsp	*sesame seeds*	15 mL
1 tbsp	*poppy seeds*	15 mL
½ tsp	*salt*	2 mL
1 tsp	*sugar*	5 mL
8 cups	*mixed salad greens*	2 L
2	*mangoes, peeled and cut into slices*	2
2 cups	*strawberries, sliced*	500 mL
1	*small red onion, sliced into rings*	1

1. To make dressing, combine oil, vinegar, lemon juice, honey, sesame seeds, poppy seeds, salt and sugar in a jar. Shake to slightly thicken. Chill.
2. Just before serving, toss salad greens with chilled dressing. Place the greens in a large bowl or on a platter.
3. Arrange sliced mangoes and strawberries on top of greens and garnish with red onion. If there is any dressing left over, sprinkle a little of it over the fruit and serve.

CORNING RECOMMENDS

PYREX® Originals™ 1-cup Measuring Cup and CORNINGWARE® Casual Elegance White Flora® 14" Oval Platter

Fragrant Basmati Rice Pilaf

Try to find genuine basmati rice for this recipe, but if you can't, Texmati rice can be used instead. These rices have a flavour that the usual white rice just can't match. **Makes 4 servings.**

2 tbsp	*unsalted butter*	30 mL
1	*small onion, diced*	1
1 tbsp	*garlic, chopped*	15 mL
1 tbsp	*ginger root, chopped*	15 mL
½ tsp	*curry powder*	2 mL
½ cup	*toasted pine nuts*, pistachios or slivered almonds*	125 mL
⅓ cup	*dried apricots, diced*	75 mL
1 ½ cups	*basmati rice*	375 mL
3 cups	*water or chicken stock, hot*	750 mL
	salt and pepper, to taste	
2 tbsp	*parsley or coriander, chopped*	30 mL

* Toast pine nuts in 350° F (180°C) oven for 6 minutes, or just starting to colour.

1. In a saucepan, melt butter. Cook onion, garlic, ginger and curry powder until soft but not brown. Stir in nuts and apricots.
2. Wash rice until water runs clear. Add to onion mixture and stir to coat rice.
3. Add hot water or stock. Bring to a boil. Cover, reduce heat and cook about 20 minutes. Remove from heat. Season with salt and pepper. Stir in parsley or coriander.

Caesar Salad

Caesar salad is the most popular salad served in restaurants. An early reference to this salad in a 1964 cookbook described it as a "man's salad". Perhaps, 35 years ago, it was thought all that raw garlic was suitable only for men! Now, we know better, because everybody loves a good Caesar — like this one. There are two musts for a good Caesar: real bacon and the best Parmesan cheese.

Makes 4 servings.

4	*strips of bacon*	4
1	*head romaine lettuce*	1
3	*garlic cloves, pressed or finely minced*	3
	salt, to taste	
1 tsp	*Worcestershire sauce*	5 mL
3 drops	*Tabasco sauce, or to taste*	3 drops
1	*egg*	1
2 tbsp	*lemon juice, freshly squeezed*	30 mL
⅓ cup	*olive oil*	75 mL
2 tbsp	*red wine vinegar*	30 mL
6 tbsp	*grated Parmesan cheese, preferably Parmigiano Reggiano*	90 mL
½ cup	*croutons (optional)*	125 mL

1. Sauté bacon until very crisp, then drain and crumble it.
2. Remove coarse outer leaves of lettuce. Wash and thoroughly dry tender inner leaves. Break into bite-size pieces.
3. Place garlic in a large (preferably) wooden salad bowl. Use a spoon to mash garlic into sides and bottom of bowl. Sprinkle salt over garlic. Mix in Worcestershire sauce and Tabasco.
4. Put egg in measuring cup and pour hot (but not boiling) water over top to cover. Allow to rest 1 minute, drain, then separate egg and add yolk to salad bowl.
5. Mix in lemon juice and olive oil. Gradually add vinegar. Do not use all of it if dressing begins to seem too runny.
6. Add Parmesan and mix thoroughly, then add lettuce and bacon. Toss and serve.

CORNING RECOMMENDS

REVERE® Copper Clad Bottom 10" Skillet and CORELLE® IMPRESSIONS® Sand Art 1-qt Serving Bowl

Rhubarb Custard Pie in Phyllo

The phyllo pastry for this pie makes an impressive presentation. Don't be afraid to try working with phyllo. It's really very easy as long as you work quickly and keep the pastry covered as you work.

Makes 8–10 servings.

6	*phyllo pastry sheets*	6
⅓ cup	*unsalted butter, melted*	75 mL
¼ cup	*water*	50 mL
3	*eggs*	3
¾ cup	*heavy cream*	175 mL
2 tbsp	*melted butter*	30 mL
2 tbsp	*flour*	30 mL
½ tsp	*cinnamon, or to taste*	2 mL
⅓ cup	*brown sugar*	75 mL
⅓ cup	*white sugar*	75 mL
4 cups	*diced rhubarb*	1 L

1. Cut phyllo pastry in half lengthwise. Combine butter and water. Working with one piece of phyllo at a time, lay the first half sheet of pastry in bottom of a 10-inch (25-cm) pie plate. Brush with melted butter and water mixture. Continue, placing 10 of the half sheets in the pan in a spoke-like fashion and brushing with butter. The sheets of pastry will hang over edge. Fold remaining two sheets in half and place in bottom to strengthen the base.
2. In a large bowl, mix together remaining ingredients. Pour into prepared shell. Fold the overhanging pieces of phyllo in towards the centre.
3. Bake at 375°F (190°C) for 45 minutes or until centre is set. Serve warm or at room temperature sprinkled with cinnamon or strawberry ice cream on the side.

CORNING RECOMMENDS

PYREX® Originals™ 1-cup Measuring Cup, PYREX® Cranberry Ovenware 9 ½" Flavor Saver™ Pie Plate, CORELLE® IMPRESSIONS® Fresh Cut Salad/Dessert Plate

White Chocolate Tart with Fruit

This is a luscious rich dessert to serve guests, especially after a lighter tasting meal of salmon or other fish.

Makes 8–10 servings.

1 ½ cups	*chocolate wafer crumbs*	375 mL
½ cup	*melted butter*	125 mL
6 oz	*white chocolate, finely chopped*	175 g
1 ¾ cups	*heavy cream*	425 mL
3 cups	*fresh fruit, such as crushed strawberries, raspberries, sliced peaches, blueberries etc.*	750 mL
	mint leaves, for garnish	

1. To make the crust, combine crumbs and butter. Press crumbs into the bottom and up the sides of a 9-inch (23 cm) tart pan or springform pan. Bake at 400°F (200°C) for 8 minutes. Remove and cool.
2. For the filling, place chopped chocolate in a mixing bowl. Bring 1½ cups (375 mL) cream to a boil. Pour cream over chocolate. Let stand 1 minute, then whisk to combine. Pour through a strainer if lumpy. Chill thoroughly until very cold. (This process can be speeded up by chilling over iced water.) Add remaining cream to mixture. Beat at medium speed until soft peaks form. Spread over cooled tart base. Refrigerate tart or freeze.
3. To serve, remove outside ring if using springform pan. Cut tart into wedges. Spoon fresh fruit over top. Garnish with mint.

CORNING RECOMMENDS

PYREX® Originals™ 1-cup Measuring Cup and PYREX® Originals™ 9" Pie Plate

Lemon Poppy Seed Cake

This cake is delicious and, when it's topped with ice cream and berries, it becomes even more so.

Makes 8 servings.

½ cup	*butter*	125 mL
1 cup + ⅓ cup	*sugar*	250 mL + 75 mL
2	*eggs*	2
1	*lemon, grated rind and juice*	1
1 ½ cups	*flour*	375 mL
1 tsp	*baking powder*	5 mL
¼ tsp	*salt*	1 mL
1 tbsp	*poppy seeds*	15 mL
½ cup	*milk*	125 mL
2 tbsp	*lemon juice*	30 mL
	berries of choice, for garnish	
	mint, for garnish	

1. Preheat oven to 350°F (180°C).
2. In a mixing bowl, cream together butter, 1 cup (250 mL) sugar, eggs, lemon juice and rind. In another bowl, sift together flour, baking powder, salt and poppy seeds. Add dry mixture to butter mixture with the milk and stir until blended.
3. Put batter into a greased and floured loaf pan and bake for 1 hour.
4. Let stand for 10 minutes then remove from pan. Mix together 2 tbsp (30 mL) lemon juice and ⅓ cup (75 mL) sugar and brush over top and sides of the warm cake. Cool.
5. Serve a slice of cake with a scoop of ice cream, berries of your choice and a sprig of mint for garnish.

Put One Away

Make double the recipe and, after baking, wrap one loaf and freeze for future use.

CORNING RECOMMENDS

PYREX® Originals™ 1-pt Measuring Cup, PYREX® Originals™ 1 ½-qt Loaf Dish and CORELLE® IMPRESSIONS® Oceanview Salad/Dessert Plate

Blueberry Cobbler

The great thing about this recipe is that you can make it with frozen blueberries all year long. When fresh berries come in, it becomes even more of a treat.
Makes 6 servings.

4 cups	*blueberries*	1 L
½ cup + 2 tbsp	*sugar*	125 mL + 30 mL
1 tsp	*lemon juice*	5 mL
1 tbsp	*cornstarch*	15 mL
1 cup	*flour*	250 mL
1 ½ tsp	*baking powder*	7 mL
¼ tsp	*salt*	1 mL
3 tbsp	*cold butter*	45 mL
½ cup	*milk*	125 mL

1. Preheat oven to 375°F (190°C).
2. In a saucepan, stir together blueberries, ½ cup (125 mL) sugar, lemon juice and cornstarch. Cook, stirring constantly, until the fruit is bubbly and thickened. Pour into a 2-qt (2-L) baking dish.
3. Combine flour, baking powder, salt and 2 tbsp (30 mL) sugar. Cut in butter until mixture is crumbly. Stir in milk until moistened.
4. Drop batter by spoonfuls into the hot fruit. Do not stir. Bake 30 minutes until topping is golden brown. Serve hot with ice cream.

CORNING RECOMMENDS

PYREX® Originals™ 1-cup Measuring Cup, CORNINGWARE® Classics™ Cookware 2-qt Blue Velvet Covered Casserole and CORELLE® IMPRESSIONS® Blue Velvet Salad/Dessert Plate

Tart Lemon Triangles

The tartness of lemon with the sweetness of fresh strawberries . . . this is a lovely conclusion to an elegant spring dinner.

Makes 12 servings.

6 tbsp	*butter*	90 mL
¼ cup	*icing sugar*	50 mL
1 cup + 3 tbsp	*flour*	250 mL + 45 mL
3	*eggs*	3
1 cup	*sugar*	250 mL
¼ cup	*lemon juice*	50 mL
1 tbsp	*finely grated lemon peel*	15 mL
	icing sugar, for garnish	
½ cup	*whipping cream*	125 mL
12	*strawberries*	12
	mint, for garnish	

1. Preheat oven to 350°F (180°C).
2. Process butter, icing sugar and 1 cup (250 mL) flour in a food processor for 10 seconds. Pat dough evenly into the bottom of a 9-inch (23 cm) pie plate. Bake for 12 to 15 minutes until lightly browned.
3. Combine eggs, sugar, lemon juice, peel and 3 tbsp (45 mL) flour in a food processor until well mixed. Pour over hot crust. Bake for 15 to 20 minutes until firm. Remove from oven and cool.
4. Sprinkle with icing sugar. Cut into 12 triangles. Whip cream. Place slices on serving plates. Put a spoonful of whipped cream on the wide part of each triangle. Top with a strawberry and a mint leaf.

CORNING RECOMMENDS

CORNINGWARE® FRENCH WHITE® 10" Pie Plate and CORELLE® IMPRESSIONS® Enhancements Salad/Dessert Plate

Index

appetizers 3-11
beef 31
beets 44
blueberry cobbler 60
brunch dishes 15, 20, 24, 40
Caesar salad 52
cake, lemon poppy seed 59
casserole dishes 12, 16, 32, 36, 40, 43, 47
cheese dishes 4, 8, 20, 36, 40
chicken 12, 23, 39
chocolate, white 56
cobbler, blueberry 60
Cornish hens 39
crostini 4
desserts 55–63
eggs 15, 20, 24, 40
fish 19
fruit 48, 55, 56, 60, 63
ham 40
lamb 35
lemon triangles 63
main courses 12–43
meat 31, 35, 40
mushrooms 4, 20, 43
pasta 16, 27, 28, 32
pie 55, 56
pizza 8
potatoes, mashed 47
quiche 15, 20
rhubarb 55
rice 43, 51
risotto 43
rub, lime herb 39
salad 3, 7, 48, 52
salad dressings 3, 4, 48, 52
sauce, horseradish 31
sauce, spicy cream 32
sauce, tartar 19
sauce, white clam 28
seafood 7, 19, 28, 36
shrimp 7, 36
side dishes 43–52
tarts, dessert 56, 63
tortillas 11, 24
vegetable dishes 11, 43, 44, 47
vegetarian dishes 3, 4, 8, 11, 15, 16, 20, 27, 44, 47, 48
wraps 11, 24

Produced exclusively for Corning Canada Inc., 60 Leek Crescent, Richmond Hill, Ontario Canada L4B 1H1 by Alpha Corporation/Susan Yates, Publisher
Photographs by Peter Paterson/Paterson Photographic Works Inc.
Copy Editor: Wendy Thomas
Editorial Services: Colborne Communications Centre
Text Cover and Design: Dave Murphy/Artplus Ltd.
Page Layout: Valerie Bateman & Leanne Knox/Artplus Ltd.
Printed and bound in Canada by Transcontinental Printing Inc.

For product information call: 905-771-3575

ISBN: 1-896391-22-2

Distributed by Canadian Tire Corporation